Copyright Page

Title of the Book

© 2024 by L. Numeris

All rights reserved. No part of this book may be reproduced, distributed, or transmitted in any form or by any means, including photocopying, recording, or other electronic or mechanical methods, without the prior written permission of the publisher, except in the case of brief quotations embodied in critical reviews and certain other noncommercial uses permitted by copyright law. For permission requests, write to the publisher at the email address below.

Publisher:

L. Numeris
Email: lnumerislotterystrategies@gmail.com

This book is a work of nonfiction. While the author has made every effort to ensure the accuracy and completeness of the information contained herein, the author assumes no responsibility for errors, inaccuracies, omissions, or any inconsistency herein.

Any references to historical events, real people, or real places are used fictitiously. Names, characters, and places mentioned in this book are the product of the author's imagination or are used fictitiously.

Chapter 1: Advanced Understanding of Lottery Mechanics

Introduction to Advanced Lottery Mechanics

The lottery, at its core, is a game of chance. However, understanding the deeper mechanics of how lottery systems work can provide serious players with insights that go beyond the basic level. This chapter dives into the structure of various lottery games, the role of randomness, and the common misconceptions that even seasoned players might hold.

Section 1: Deep Dive into Lottery Systems

- 1.1 Popular Lottery Formats

Lotteries come in various forms, each with its own set of rules, odds, and potential rewards. Understanding these differences is crucial for choosing the right lottery to play and optimizing your strategy.

- Single-State vs. Multi-State Lotteries:
  Single-state lotteries, like the Florida Lottery, are restricted to residents of that state, typically offering smaller jackpots but better odds compared to multi-state lotteries. On the other hand, multi-state lotteries like Mega Millions or Powerball pool entries from multiple states, leading to much larger jackpots but with significantly lower odds of winning.

- Draw-Based Games vs. Instant Win (Scratch-Offs):
  Draw-based games involve selecting numbers and waiting for a scheduled draw to see if you've won. These games are generally the focus of long-term strategies due to their structured nature and jackpot potential. Scratch-off games, in contrast, offer instant results and usually smaller prizes. They require a different approach, often focusing on understanding the odds of different ticket batches.

- Online Lotteries:
  With the rise of digital platforms, online lotteries have become more popular. These allow players to participate in international lotteries or online-exclusive games, often with innovative formats and varying odds. However, players must be cautious about ensuring they are participating in legitimate and legal lotteries.

Understanding these formats allows you to tailor your approach. For example, if your goal is frequent smaller wins, a single-state lottery or scratch-off games may be more appropriate. For those chasing life-changing sums, multi-state lotteries or select international lotteries might be the focus.

- 1.2 The Role of Randomness in Lottery Draws

Lottery draws are designed to be random, ensuring fairness and unpredictability. However, the way randomness is implemented can vary between different lotteries.

- Random Number Generators (RNGs) vs. Traditional Ball Draws:
  Traditional ball machines, used in many major lotteries, involve physical balls being randomly selected. The design and operation of these machines are strictly controlled to prevent any bias. On the other hand, RNGs, which are used in many digital and some smaller lotteries, use complex algorithms to generate numbers. While both methods aim to produce equally random results, some players feel more confident in the transparency of physical ball draws.

- Statistical Independence:
  Each lottery draw is independent of the previous one, meaning that past results do not influence future draws. This concept, known as statistical independence, is fundamental in understanding that while patterns might emerge over time, they don't indicate a "due" number or guarantee any future outcomes.

Understanding the true randomness of lottery draws is crucial in avoiding common fallacies, such as the belief that a number that hasn't been drawn in a while is "due" to appear soon.

- 1.3 How Jackpot Sizes Affect Player Behavior

Jackpot size significantly influences player behavior, often leading to changes in strategy, ticket sales, and even the odds of winning.

- The Psychology of Jackpot Size:
  As jackpots grow, more players are enticed to buy tickets, often leading to a phenomenon known as "jackpot fever." This influx of new players can make the odds of sharing a jackpot higher, even though the odds of winning remain the same. Understanding this can help you decide whether it's worth playing during these peak times or if it's better to focus on smaller, less competitive jackpots.

- Impact of Rollovers:
  Rollovers, where the jackpot is carried over to the next draw if there's no winner, lead to larger prizes but also increased ticket sales. Players need to weigh the appeal of a larger prize against the increased competition. For some, it might be more strategic to play when jackpots are smaller, reducing the number of tickets sold and slightly improving the odds of a solo win.

Strategic players often analyze these factors to determine the optimal time to play, considering both the size of the prize and the level of competition.

Section 2: Probability and Advanced Odds Calculation

- 2.1 Understanding Odds and Probability

The foundation of any lottery strategy is a solid understanding of probability and how it applies to different games.

- **Basic Probability Concepts:**
  In lotteries, probability is often expressed as the odds of winning, such as 1 in 292 million for Powerball. This represents the number of possible combinations that can be drawn versus the single winning combination.

  - **Permutations vs. Combinations:**
    Permutations account for the order in which numbers are drawn, while combinations do not. Since most lotteries only care about which numbers are chosen, not the order, understanding combinations is key. For example, the number of ways to choose 5 numbers from a set of 50 is calculated using combinations, not permutations.

- **Calculating Odds for Different Games:**
  Each lottery game has its own odds, depending on the number of numbers players must choose and the size of the pool of possible numbers. Calculating these odds helps players understand the likelihood of winning different prize tiers. For example, while the odds of hitting the jackpot in Powerball are extremely low, the odds of winning a smaller prize, such as matching three numbers, are significantly better.

Understanding these basic concepts allows players to make informed decisions about which games to play and what strategies might give them the best chance of winning.

- 2.2 Conditional Probability in Lottery Play

Conditional probability involves calculating the probability of an event, given that another event has occurred. This concept can be applied to lotteries in various ways.

- **Applying Conditional Probability:**
  For instance, in lotteries where bonus numbers or additional draws are involved, conditional probability can help players assess the likelihood of winning different prize tiers based on previous results.

  - **Case Studies:**
    Consider a lottery where a bonus ball is drawn after the main numbers. By understanding the relationship between the main draw and the bonus draw, players can better estimate their chances of winning secondary prizes, which often have better odds than the jackpot.

Conditional probability adds another layer of strategy, especially in games with multiple stages or prize levels.

- 2.3 Misunderstanding Probability: Common Pitfalls

Many players fall into traps due to a poor understanding of probability. Recognizing and avoiding these mistakes is crucial.

- Cognitive Biases in Lottery Play:
  Players often succumb to biases such as the Gambler's Fallacy, which is the belief that if something happens more frequently than normal during a given period, it will happen less frequently in the future (or vice versa). In reality, each lottery draw is independent, and past results do not influence future outcomes.

  - Hot-Hand Fallacy:
    This is the mistaken belief that a number that has been "hot" or frequently drawn recently will continue to be drawn. In fact, in a random draw, all numbers have an equal chance of being selected, regardless of their past frequency.

- Avoiding Common Errors:
  By understanding these biases and errors, players can make more rational, informed decisions, rather than relying on misconceptions or "gut feelings" that don't align with the mathematics of the game.

Understanding and avoiding these pitfalls is key to maintaining a disciplined and effective lottery strategy.

Section 3: Misconceptions Among Experienced Players

- 3.1 Debunking Common Myths

Even seasoned players can fall prey to myths that undermine their strategies.

- The Myth of "Due Numbers":
  A common belief is that numbers that haven't been drawn for a long time are "due" to come up. However, due to the independence of each draw, this belief is statistically unfounded. Every number has an equal chance of being drawn in each game, regardless of when it was last drawn.

- The Fallacy of Lucky Numbers:
  Many players have "lucky" numbers they consistently play. While this can be a fun and personal way to engage with the lottery, it doesn't improve the odds. Relying too heavily on personal significance can lead to less strategic number selection.

Debunking these myths helps players approach the lottery with a clear, rational mindset, improving their chances of making decisions based on sound strategy rather than superstition.

- 3.2 Advanced Misconceptions: Even Experienced Players Get It Wrong

Even players who understand the basics can fall into advanced traps.

- Case Studies of Misguided Strategies:
  Examples of experienced players who misunderstood probability, relied too heavily on past patterns, or failed to adapt their strategies to new information can provide valuable lessons. These cases highlight the importance of continual learning and the dangers of becoming too comfortable with any one approach.

- Challenging Assumptions:
  The best lottery players constantly question their strategies, testing assumptions and adapting to new insights. This flexibility is key to long-term success.

Understanding that even experienced players can make mistakes reinforces the need for continual learning and adaptation.

- 3.3 The Importance of Continual Learning

The lottery landscape is always evolving, and so should your strategies.

- Staying Informed:
  New lottery formats, changes in regulations, and advances in statistical analysis mean that there is always more to learn. Serious players should regularly review their strategies, learn from others, and stay informed about developments in the world of lotteries.

- Resources for Ongoing Education:
  Books, online courses, and forums can be invaluable resources

Chapter 2: Analyzing Historical Data

Introduction to Analyzing Historical Lottery Data

For serious lottery players, analyzing historical data is a crucial aspect of developing a successful strategy. While the lottery is inherently random, patterns and trends can sometimes be observed over time. By studying past draws, players can make more informed decisions about which numbers to play. This chapter will guide you through the process of analyzing lottery data, identifying meaningful patterns, and applying these insights to enhance your chances of winning.

Section 1: The Value of Historical Lottery Data

- 1.1 Why Analyze Historical Data?

Analyzing historical lottery data allows players to identify trends that might not be immediately obvious. While the odds of any specific combination of numbers being drawn remain the same, certain patterns can emerge that, when understood correctly, might give you a slight edge.

- Identifying Potential Patterns:
  Historical data analysis helps to spot trends like numbers that tend to be drawn together, numbers that haven't appeared for a long time, or sequences that seem to repeat. Though randomness dictates that no number is truly "due," analyzing patterns can inform your strategy by highlighting trends that have occurred in the past.

- Understanding the Role of Randomness:
  While analyzing historical data, it's essential to remember that lotteries are designed to be random. Any observed patterns are coincidental, not predictive. However, understanding how randomness manifests over time can provide insights into which strategies might be worth exploring further.

- 1.2 Tools and Resources for Data Analysis

To effectively analyze historical lottery data, you'll need the right tools and resources. Fortunately, a variety of software and online tools are available to assist in this endeavor.

- Spreadsheet Software (e.g., Excel, Google Sheets):
  Spreadsheets are versatile tools for organizing and analyzing data. You can use them to track draw results, calculate frequencies, and visualize patterns over time. With functions like COUNTIF and SUM, you can quickly tally how often each number appears and analyze their distribution.

- Dedicated Lottery Analysis Software:
  Several specialized software packages are designed specifically for lottery analysis. These tools often include features such as number tracking, frequency analysis, and pattern detection. Some of the more advanced programs even allow for the simulation of different strategies, helping you to test and refine your approach.

- Online Databases and Tools:
  Many lottery websites offer historical draw data, often going back several years. These databases can be invaluable for players looking to analyze trends over time. Additionally, online tools and calculators can assist with everything from calculating odds to generating wheeling systems based on historical data.

- 1.3 Recognizing the Limits of Data Analysis

While analyzing historical data can be a powerful tool, it's important to recognize its limitations.

- The Random Nature of Lotteries:
  Lotteries are designed to be random, and while patterns can be observed, they don't guarantee future outcomes. Relying too heavily on historical data can lead to overconfidence, which can be detrimental to your overall strategy.

- Statistical Significance:
  Not all patterns are statistically significant. It's important to differentiate between meaningful trends and random noise. For example, a number appearing more frequently over a short period may be nothing more than a statistical anomaly rather than a predictive pattern.

- Balancing Data Analysis with Other Strategies:
  While historical data analysis is an important part of a comprehensive lottery strategy, it should be balanced with other approaches. Combining data-driven insights with techniques like wheeling systems and probability analysis can lead to a more robust strategy.

Section 2: Identifying Patterns and Trends

- 2.1 Hot and Cold Numbers

The concepts of "hot" and "cold" numbers are among the most commonly discussed topics in lottery strategy. Understanding these concepts and how to use them effectively can provide valuable insights.

- Defining Hot and Cold Numbers:
  Hot numbers are those that have been drawn frequently within a given period, while cold numbers are those that have been drawn less frequently or not at all. Some players believe that hot numbers are more likely to be drawn again, while others favor cold numbers, assuming they are "due" for a draw.

- Statistical Analysis of Hot and Cold Numbers:
  To determine whether a number is genuinely hot or cold, you can analyze its frequency over time. This involves calculating the average frequency of each number and comparing it to its actual frequency. However, it's crucial to remember that each draw is independent, so a hot or cold number has the same chance of being drawn as any other.

- Strategies for Using Hot and Cold Numbers:
  Players who use hot numbers often focus on those that have appeared multiple times in recent draws, believing that momentum will continue. Conversely, those who favor cold numbers might choose them based on the idea that these numbers are "due" to appear. Both approaches have their merits, but they should be applied cautiously and as part of a broader strategy.

- ## 2.2 Number Frequency Analysis

Frequency analysis involves examining how often each number has been drawn over a set period. This analysis can reveal trends and patterns that might inform your number selection process.

- **Conducting a Frequency Analysis:**
  Start by compiling a list of past draws and tallying how often each number has been drawn. Once you have this data, you can calculate the relative frequency of each number, allowing you to identify which numbers appear most and least often.

- **Significance of High-Frequency Numbers:**
  High-frequency numbers are those that have appeared more often than others. Some players believe these numbers are more likely to appear again, while others avoid them, thinking they are overrepresented and less likely to be drawn in the future.

- **Practical Examples of Frequency Analysis:**
  For example, if a particular number has appeared in 10% of the last 100 draws, you might consider including it in your selection. However, it's important to balance this with an understanding of randomness, ensuring that your strategy isn't solely dependent on frequency analysis.

- ## 2.3 Clustering and Number Grouping

Number clustering refers to the phenomenon where certain numbers tend to appear together more often than others. Understanding this concept can help in choosing groups of numbers that might increase your chances of winning.

- **Understanding Number Clustering:**
  Clustering occurs when certain numbers appear together more frequently than would be expected by chance. This could be due to the way the lottery is drawn or simply random occurrence. Identifying these clusters can help players choose numbers that have historically appeared together.

- **The Concept of Number Grouping:**
  Number grouping involves selecting groups of numbers based on observed clusters. For example, if the numbers 7, 14, and 21 have frequently appeared together in past draws, a player might choose to include these numbers in a single ticket.

- **Case Studies of Clustering and Grouping:**
  Historical examples of clustering and number grouping can provide insight into how these strategies have been successfully employed. By analyzing these cases, players can develop a more nuanced approach to selecting numbers.

Section 3: Applying Data Analysis to Your Strategy

- 3.1 Integrating Data into Your Number Selection

Once you've analyzed historical data, the next step is to integrate these insights into your number selection strategy.

- Using Data to Inform Your Choices:
  By combining data-driven insights with other strategies, you can make more informed decisions about which numbers to play. For example, if your analysis shows that certain numbers frequently cluster together, you might choose to include those numbers in a single ticket.

- Balancing Data with Random Selection:
  While data analysis can provide valuable insights, it's important to balance this with an element of randomness. This approach ensures that you're not over-relying on any one strategy, which can be risky.

- Examples of Data-Driven Number Selection:
  Players who have successfully integrated data analysis into their strategies often use a combination of hot numbers, frequency analysis, and clustering to inform their selections. These examples can serve as a guide for developing your own approach.

- 3.2 Avoiding Over-Reliance on Historical Data

While historical data analysis is a powerful tool, it's essential not to rely too heavily on it.

- The Risks of Over-Reliance:
  Over-reliance on historical data can lead to complacency and overconfidence. It's important to remember that the lottery is ultimately a game of chance, and no amount of data can predict future outcomes with certainty.

- Maintaining Flexibility in Your Strategy:
  To avoid over-reliance, ensure that your strategy remains flexible and adaptable. This might involve regularly reassessing your approach, incorporating new data, and staying open to other strategies.

- The Importance of a Dynamic Strategy:
  A successful lottery strategy is one that evolves over time. By continually refining your approach based on new information and experiences, you can improve your chances of success.

- 3.3 Case Studies: Successes and Failures

Studying the successes and failures of others can provide valuable lessons for your own lottery play.

- **Examples of Successful Data-Driven Strategies:**
  Case studies of players who have successfully used data analysis to win significant prizes can provide inspiration and guidance. These examples show how data-driven strategies can be effectively applied in real-world situations.

- **Learning from Mistakes:**
  Conversely, examining the failures of others can help you avoid common pitfalls. Understanding why certain strategies didn't work can inform your own approach and help you steer clear of similar mistakes.

- **Applying These Lessons to Your Strategy:**
  By learning from both successes and failures, you can develop a more robust and effective lottery strategy. The key is to remain adaptable, continually refining your approach based on what works and what doesn't.

Conclusion of Chapter 2

Analyzing historical lottery data is a powerful tool that, when used correctly, can provide valuable insights into the patterns and trends that might influence your number selection. While it's essential to recognize the inherent randomness of lotteries, understanding and applying these data-driven strategies can give you an edge over players who rely solely on intuition or luck. By integrating data analysis into your broader lottery strategy, you can make more informed decisions and improve your overall chances of success.

Whether you're tracking hot and cold numbers, analyzing frequency data, or exploring number clustering, the key is to balance these insights with a healthy understanding of the lottery's random nature. Avoid over-reliance on any single approach, and remain flexible and adaptable as you refine your strategy over time.

This chapter has provided you with the tools and knowledge needed to effectively analyze historical data and apply it to your lottery play. As you move forward, continue to explore and experiment with different methods, always seeking to improve your strategy and enhance your chances of winning.

Chapter 3: Advanced Number Selection Strategies

Introduction to Advanced Number Selection Strategies

Selecting the right numbers is one of the most critical aspects of any lottery strategy. While many players rely on random selection or personal numbers, serious players understand the value of a more strategic approach. This chapter delves into advanced techniques for choosing lottery numbers, including wheeling systems, combinatorial math, and strategies for balancing risk and reward. By applying these methods, you can increase your chances of securing a win while managing the inherent risks of lottery play.

Section 1: Wheeling Systems and Their Applications

- 1.1 Introduction to Number Wheeling

Number wheeling is a strategy used by serious lottery players to maximize their coverage of potential winning combinations. By organizing your number choices into a systematic pattern, wheeling can increase your chances of hitting multiple numbers in a draw.

- What is Number Wheeling?
  Number wheeling involves selecting a larger set of numbers and then playing all possible combinations of those numbers in smaller groups. For example, if you select 10 numbers, a wheeling system might create multiple tickets that each cover a subset of those numbers in various combinations.

- Why Use Wheeling Systems?
  The primary advantage of wheeling systems is that they allow you to cover more combinations, which can increase your chances of matching several numbers in a draw. This approach is particularly useful for players who participate in syndicates or who are willing to invest in multiple tickets.

- 1.2 Types of Wheeling Systems

There are several types of wheeling systems, each with its own benefits and trade-offs. Choosing the right system depends on your budget, risk tolerance, and the specific lottery game you're playing.

- Full Wheels:
  Full wheeling systems generate all possible combinations of your selected numbers. For example, if you choose 10 numbers and need to match 6 to win, a full wheel will create tickets covering every possible combination of 6 numbers out of the 10. While this maximizes coverage, it can also be costly, as the number of tickets required increases exponentially with the number of selected numbers.

- Abbreviated Wheels:
  Abbreviated wheeling systems reduce the number of tickets needed by focusing on specific combinations that are more likely to win. While this approach doesn't cover all possible combinations, it strikes a balance between coverage and cost, making it more accessible to players with limited budgets.

- Key Number Wheels:
  In key number wheeling, you designate one or more "key" numbers that you believe are most likely to be drawn. These key numbers are included in every ticket, while the other numbers rotate. This method reduces the total number of combinations while still ensuring that your key numbers are always in play.

- 1.3 Practical Application of Wheeling Systems

To effectively use a wheeling system, it's essential to understand how to implement it within your overall strategy.

- Step-by-Step Guide to Using Wheeling Systems:
  Start by selecting your set of numbers based on your analysis of historical data, frequency, or other factors. Next, choose the type of wheeling system that best suits your budget and strategy. Use lottery software or wheeling tools to generate the combinations, and then purchase the necessary tickets.

- Real-Life Examples of Wheeling Systems:
  Many lottery winners have attributed their success to wheeling systems. For instance, a group of 16 employees in New York won a $56 million Mega Millions jackpot using an abbreviated wheeling system. By pooling their resources, they were able to cover more combinations, significantly increasing their chances of winning.

- Tools and Software for Wheeling Systems:
  Numerous software programs and online tools are available to help you create and manage wheeling systems. These tools can automatically generate the necessary combinations, track your tickets, and even optimize your selections based on your budget and the specific lottery game you're playing.

Section 2: Using Combinatorial Math for Number Selection

- 2.1 Introduction to Combinatorial Math

Combinatorial math is a branch of mathematics that deals with combinations and permutations. In the context of lottery play, it provides a framework for understanding the relationships between different sets of numbers and optimizing your selections.

- The Basics of Combinatorial Mathematics:
  In lottery games, players are typically asked to select a certain number of numbers from a larger pool (e.g., 6 numbers out of 49). Combinatorial math helps you calculate the total number of possible combinations and identify the most promising subsets of numbers to play.

- Permutations vs. Combinations:
  Permutations consider the order of numbers, while combinations do not. Since most lotteries only care about which numbers are chosen, not the order in which they are drawn, understanding combinations is crucial. For example, the number of ways to choose 6 numbers from a pool of 49 can be calculated using the combination formula, which helps in determining the odds of winning.

- 2.2 Applying Combinatorial Strategies

By applying combinatorial principles, you can create more balanced and optimized number sets, increasing your chances of winning.

- Creating Balanced Number Sets:
  A common combinatorial strategy is to create balanced number sets that evenly distribute low and high numbers, odd and even numbers, or other relevant criteria. This approach increases the likelihood that your chosen set will align with the numbers drawn in a given lottery.

- Optimizing Combinations:
  Once you understand the total number of possible combinations, you can start optimizing your selections by eliminating less likely combinations (e.g., all even numbers) and focusing on those that have a higher probability of matching the draw. This optimization can be done manually or using lottery software that incorporates combinatorial algorithms.

- Examples of Combinatorial Strategies:
  For example, in a game where you must select 6 numbers out of 49, you might use a combinatorial strategy to ensure that your chosen numbers include an even mix of low and high numbers, which statistically have a better chance of winning. Many lottery players have used these strategies to improve their odds, leading to significant wins.

- 2.3 Advanced Combinatorial Techniques

For those looking to take their lottery play to the next level, advanced combinatorial techniques offer even greater potential for optimizing your strategy.

- Exploring Complex Combinatorial Strategies:
  Advanced techniques might involve using statistical analysis to identify subsets of numbers that have historically performed well together or applying probability theory to refine your number selections further.

- Blending Combinatorial Methods with Other Strategies:
  Combining combinatorial techniques with wheeling systems, historical data analysis, or frequency studies can create a more comprehensive strategy. For instance, you might use combinatorial methods to select your numbers and then apply a wheeling system to maximize coverage.

- Adapting to Different Lottery Formats:
  Different lotteries have different rules, and it's important to adapt your combinatorial strategy accordingly. For example, a game with a bonus ball might require a different approach than one without, as the additional number can significantly affect the odds and possible combinations.

Section 3: Balancing Risk and Reward in Number Selection

- 3.1 Understanding Risk in Lottery Play

Every lottery strategy involves a balance of risk and reward. Understanding this balance is key to creating a successful number selection strategy.

- **Assessing the Risk Level of Different Combinations:**
  Some combinations are riskier than others, either because they include numbers that are statistically less likely to be drawn or because they rely on patterns that have not been successful in the past. By assessing the risk level of your chosen combinations, you can make more informed decisions about which numbers to play.

- **Strategies for Choosing High-Risk vs. Low-Risk Combinations:**
  High-risk combinations might involve selecting all low numbers, all high numbers, or all odd or even numbers. While these combinations are less likely to be drawn, they offer a higher reward if they do. Conversely, low-risk combinations involve a more balanced selection of numbers, which may offer smaller but more consistent rewards.

- 3.2 Psychological Factors in Number Selection

The psychology of decision-making plays a significant role in lottery play. Understanding these psychological factors can help you make more rational, strategic choices.

- **Cognitive Biases in Number Selection:**
  Players often fall prey to cognitive biases, such as overestimating the likelihood of a particular pattern or relying too heavily on past results. Recognizing these biases can help you avoid common pitfalls and make more objective decisions.

- **The Role of Intuition vs. Analysis:**
  Many players rely on intuition when selecting numbers, choosing those that "feel" right or have personal significance. While intuition can be a powerful tool, it should be balanced with rigorous analysis to ensure that your selections are based on sound strategy rather than emotion.

- **Overcoming Biases and Making Rational Decisions:**
  By combining data analysis, combinatorial math, and a clear understanding of the risks involved, you can overcome cognitive biases and make more rational, informed decisions about your number selection.

- 3.3 Creating a Balanced Number Selection Strategy

The key to successful lottery play is creating a strategy that balances risk and reward while remaining flexible and adaptable.

- Combining Wheeling, Combinatorial Math, and Risk Assessment:
By integrating wheeling systems, combinatorial techniques, and risk assessment into your strategy, you can create a comprehensive approach that maximizes your chances of winning. This balanced strategy should be regularly reviewed and adjusted based on your results and any new information you acquire.

- Staying Adaptable and Open to New Approaches:
The lottery is constantly evolving, and so should your strategy. Staying adaptable and open to new techniques, tools, and insights will help you maintain a competitive edge and increase your chances of success. Regularly reassess your strategy in light of new information, such as changes in lottery formats, new research on lottery probabilities, or shifts in your personal financial situation. Flexibility is key to ensuring that your strategy remains effective over time.

- Case Studies of Successful Balanced Strategies:

Reviewing real-life examples of lottery winners who successfully balanced risk and reward can provide valuable insights. For instance, consider the case of a lottery syndicate that combined conservative and aggressive strategies, such as using a wheeling system with a mix of high-frequency and low-frequency numbers. By strategically balancing their approach, they managed to maximize their chances of winning without overextending their resources.

Another example could involve a solo player who focused on low-risk combinations for steady, smaller wins while occasionally placing a high-risk, high-reward bet. This approach allowed the player to maintain financial stability while still participating in the lottery with the potential for a significant windfall.

These case studies illustrate the importance of creating a balanced strategy that aligns with your goals, risk tolerance, and resources. By learning from the experiences of others, you can refine your approach and improve your chances of success.

Conclusion of Chapter 3

Advanced number selection strategies are essential tools for serious lottery players who seek to enhance their chances of winning. By mastering wheeling systems, combinatorial math, and the delicate balance between risk and reward, you can create a well-rounded approach that increases your odds of success while managing the inherent risks of lottery play.

The key to success lies in combining these strategies in a way that suits your individual preferences and circumstances. Whether you prefer a conservative approach with low-risk combinations or are willing to take calculated risks with more aggressive strategies, the techniques outlined in this chapter provide a solid foundation for making informed, strategic decisions.

As you move forward, remember that flexibility and continual learning are crucial. The lottery landscape is always changing, and your strategy should evolve with it. By staying adaptable, informed, and disciplined, you can maintain a competitive edge and improve your overall chances of hitting that elusive jackpot.

Chapter 4: Maximizing Your Chances with Group Play

Introduction to Group Play and Lottery Syndicates

Playing the lottery as part of a group, also known as a syndicate, is a popular strategy that can significantly improve your chances of winning. By pooling resources, you can purchase more tickets and cover more number combinations, effectively increasing the likelihood of hitting a winning combination. However, group play also comes with its own set of challenges, including the need for clear agreements and financial management. This chapter explores the advantages of group play, detailed strategies for optimizing your syndicate's chances, and important legal and financial considerations.

Section 1: Detailed Strategies for Syndicates

- 1.1 Understanding Lottery Syndicates

A lottery syndicate is a group of players who pool their money to buy multiple lottery tickets. The idea is simple: by purchasing more tickets as a group, you increase your chances of winning. If one of the tickets wins, the prize is divided among the members of the syndicate according to pre-agreed terms.

- How Syndicates Work:
  In a typical syndicate, each member contributes a set amount of money to buy tickets. The more members there are, the more tickets can be purchased, and the greater the coverage of possible number combinations. This approach spreads the risk and the reward among all participants.

- Advantages of Joining or Forming a Syndicate:
  The primary advantage of a syndicate is the improved odds of winning. Even though you may have to share the prize, the likelihood of winning something is higher than if you were playing alone. Additionally, syndicates allow players to participate in larger, more expensive wheeling systems that would be cost-prohibitive for an individual.

- Challenges and Considerations:
  While syndicates can be highly effective, they also require clear communication, trust, and legal agreements to avoid disputes. It's important to have well-defined rules about how contributions are made, how winnings are distributed, and what happens if a member fails to contribute.

- 1.2 Setting Up a Successful Syndicate

To maximize the benefits of a lottery syndicate, it's crucial to set it up correctly from the start. This involves careful planning, clear agreements, and effective management.

- Forming a Syndicate:
  The first step in setting up a syndicate is to gather a group of like-minded players. This group could be made up of friends, family, or colleagues. It's important that everyone involved is committed to the same goals and understands the rules of the syndicate.

- Roles and Responsibilities:
  Clear roles should be established within the syndicate. Typically, one person acts as the organizer, responsible for collecting contributions, purchasing tickets, and managing communication. An accountant or treasurer role can also be designated to handle the financial aspects, ensuring that all contributions and winnings are accounted for.

- Establishing Rules and Agreements:
  Before purchasing any tickets, the syndicate should create a formal agreement that outlines the rules. This agreement should cover how much each member contributes, how often contributions are made, how tickets are purchased, and how winnings are distributed. It should also address what happens if a member fails to contribute on time or decides to leave the syndicate.

↓

- 1.3 Optimizing Number Selection in Group Play

One of the key benefits of a syndicate is the ability to play more number combinations, but this advantage can be maximized with strategic number selection.

- Choosing Numbers Strategically:
  Syndicates have the advantage of purchasing more tickets, allowing for broader coverage of possible combinations. However, it's important to avoid duplicating numbers across multiple tickets to ensure that the syndicate's resources are used as efficiently as possible. Strategies such as wheeling systems can be particularly effective in group play.

- Avoiding Duplicate Selections:
  To maximize coverage, syndicates should ensure that the numbers chosen across different tickets do not overlap unnecessarily. This can be achieved by using lottery software that tracks selections and ensures that each ticket covers a unique combination of numbers.

- Case Studies of Successful Syndicates:
  Many syndicates have won significant prizes by applying these principles. For example, a group of Australian healthcare workers won $40 million in a Powerball syndicate by carefully selecting numbers and using a wheeling system to maximize their coverage. By learning from these success stories, you can apply similar strategies to your syndicate.

Section 2: Legal and Financial Considerations for Syndicates

- 2.1 Legal Framework for Lottery Syndicates

Operating a lottery syndicate comes with legal responsibilities that must be understood and addressed to avoid potential disputes and complications.

- Understanding the Legalities:
  The legal framework governing lottery syndicates can vary depending on the jurisdiction. In some regions, syndicates are required to register, while in others, informal agreements between members may suffice. It's important to understand the laws in your area to ensure that your syndicate operates legally.

- Creating a Syndicate Agreement:
  A well-drafted syndicate agreement is essential to prevent disputes and protect all members. This agreement should be in writing and signed by all members. It should outline the contributions required, the process for purchasing tickets, how winnings are distributed, and the procedures for handling any disputes.

- Jurisdictional Differences:
  Legal requirements for syndicates can vary widely between different countries, states, or provinces. For example, some jurisdictions may require that syndicates be registered with the lottery authority, while others may have specific rules about the taxation of winnings. Understanding these differences is crucial for ensuring that your syndicate complies with all relevant laws.

- 2.2 Financial Management within a Syndicate

Effective financial management is crucial to the success of a syndicate. This includes managing contributions, purchasing tickets, and distributing winnings.

- Managing Contributions:
  It's important to establish a clear process for collecting contributions from all members. Contributions should be collected well in advance of ticket purchases to ensure that the syndicate has sufficient funds. It's also essential to keep detailed records of all contributions to avoid any disputes.

- Handling Winnings:
  Once a win is secured, the syndicate must have a clear process for distributing the prize money. This process should be outlined in the syndicate agreement and followed meticulously. All members should receive their share of the winnings according to the terms of the agreement, and the distribution should be documented.

- Tax Implications:
  Depending on the jurisdiction, lottery winnings may be subject to taxation. In some cases, the syndicate itself may be responsible for withholding and remitting taxes before distributing the winnings. It's important to consult with a tax professional to ensure that all tax obligations are met.

- 2.3 Protecting Your Syndicate's Interests

To safeguard the interests of all members, it's important to implement measures that ensure transparency, fairness, and legal compliance.

- Legal Protections:
  The syndicate agreement should include clauses that protect the interests of all members, such as dispute resolution mechanisms and procedures for handling breaches of the agreement. It's also wise to consult with a lawyer when drafting the agreement to ensure that it complies with local laws and effectively protects all parties involved.

- Ensuring Transparency:
  Transparency is key to maintaining trust within the syndicate. All members should have access to information about contributions, ticket purchases, and winnings. Regular communication and clear record-keeping are essential to ensure that everyone is on the same page.

- Steps to Take if Conflicts Arise:
  Despite the best planning, conflicts can still arise within a syndicate. It's important to have a process in place for resolving disputes quickly and fairly. This may include mediation or arbitration, as outlined in the syndicate agreement. Having a clear process for addressing issues can prevent conflicts from escalating and ensure that the syndicate remains harmonious.

Section 3: Advanced Group Play Techniques

- 3.1 Innovative Approaches to Pooling Resources

Beyond traditional syndicates, there are innovative approaches to group play that can further enhance your chances of winning.

- Syndicate Wheeling:
  One advanced technique involves using wheeling systems within a syndicate to maximize the coverage of number combinations. By pooling resources, the syndicate can afford to use more comprehensive wheeling systems, which would be prohibitively expensive for individual players.

- Leveraging Technology:
  Technology can play a significant role in managing a syndicate more effectively. Apps and software designed for lottery syndicates can automate many aspects of group play, such as tracking contributions, generating numbers, and managing tickets. These tools can also provide real-time updates on draw results and winnings, making the process more efficient and transparent.

- Unconventional Group Play Methods:
  Some syndicates take innovative approaches, such as joining forces with other syndicates to create "super syndicates" or using statistical analysis to inform group decision-making. These methods can further increase the group's chances of winning, though they may require more sophisticated planning and management.

- 3.2 Combining Group Play with Other Strategies

Group play can be even more effective when combined with individual strategies and other lottery techniques.

- Balancing Syndicate and Individual Play:
  Many players participate in both syndicates and individual play, using different strategies for each. For example, you might use a more conservative approach in your syndicate while taking higher risks with your individual tickets. This allows you to diversify your strategies and increase your overall chances of winning.

- Integrating Data Analysis into Syndicate Play:

    Just as individual players can benefit from data analysis, so too can syndicates. By analyzing historical data, frequency patterns, and other relevant information, a syndicate can make more informed decisions about which numbers to play. This data-driven approach can enhance the effectiveness of your syndicate, ensuring that the group is not just relying on random number selection but is using a strategic approach to improve its odds.

    Case Studies of Syndicates Balancing Multiple Strategies:
    Consider the example of a syndicate that used both historical data analysis and a wheeling system to maximize its chances. The group carefully selected numbers based on their frequency in past draws, then applied a wheeling system to cover a broad range of combinations. This approach allowed them to win smaller prizes consistently while also positioning them for a potential jackpot. Learning from such examples can help your syndicate develop a well-rounded strategy that balances different methods for optimal results.

- 3.3 Scaling Up: Large Syndicates vs. Small Groups

    The size of your syndicate can significantly impact its effectiveness. While larger syndicates have more resources, smaller groups offer more flexibility and higher individual payouts.

    Advantages and Disadvantages of Large Syndicates:
    Large syndicates have the advantage of being able to pool substantial resources, allowing them to purchase more tickets and cover more number combinations. However, the downside is that any winnings must be divided among more members, reducing the individual share of the prize. Additionally, managing a large syndicate can be more complex, requiring more sophisticated organization and communication.

    Benefits of Small Groups:
    Smaller syndicates, on the other hand, offer the advantage of fewer participants, meaning each member receives a larger portion of any winnings. They are also easier to manage, with less risk of disputes and simpler logistics. However, smaller groups have fewer resources, which may limit the number of tickets they can purchase and, therefore, the coverage of possible combinations.

    Examples of Large and Small Syndicate Wins:
    Historical examples show that both large and small syndicates have won significant prizes. For instance, a large syndicate in the UK won a £66 million EuroMillions jackpot, but each of the 33 members received a smaller share. In contrast, a small group of seven friends in the US won a $319 million Mega Millions jackpot, with each member taking home a substantial sum. These examples illustrate that both large and small syndicates can be successful, depending on how they are managed and the strategies they employ.

Conclusion of Chapter 4

Group play through lottery syndicates offers a powerful way to improve your chances of winning without drastically increasing your financial risk. By pooling resources and leveraging strategic number selection methods, syndicates can cover a broader range of combinations, thereby increasing the odds of success. However, the effectiveness of a syndicate depends on careful planning, clear agreements, and strategic management.

Whether you're part of a large syndicate with extensive resources or a small, tight-knit group, the key to success lies in balancing these advantages with the challenges of group play. By integrating advanced techniques, such as wheeling systems, data analysis, and strategic planning, your syndicate can maximize its potential and increase the likelihood of a significant win.

As you move forward, remember that transparency, legal compliance, and effective communication are essential to maintaining a successful syndicate. With the right approach, group play can be a rewarding and enjoyable way to participate in the lottery, offering both camaraderie and an improved chance of winning.

Chapter 5: Financial Planning and Risk Management for Lottery Players

Introduction to Financial Planning and Risk Management

Winning the lottery is a life-changing event, but it also comes with significant financial responsibilities and risks. Without proper planning, many lottery winners find themselves struggling to manage their newfound wealth, sometimes losing it all within a few years. This chapter focuses on advanced financial planning strategies and risk management techniques to ensure that your lottery winnings lead to long-term financial security and success.

Section 1: Advanced Budgeting Strategies

- 1.1 Setting a Lottery Budget

Before you win the lottery, it's crucial to maintain a disciplined approach to how much you spend on tickets. Proper budgeting ensures that you don't spend more than you can afford, preserving your financial stability regardless of whether or not you win.

- The Importance of a Lottery Budget:
  Setting a budget for lottery play is essential to avoid the pitfalls of overspending. It's easy to get caught up in the excitement of big jackpots, but without a budget, you risk spending more than you can afford, which can lead to financial strain and stress.

- Determining Your Lottery Budget:
  To determine your budget, start by reviewing your overall financial situation. Assess your income, expenses, and savings goals to see how much you can realistically allocate to lottery play without jeopardizing your financial health. A general rule of thumb is to only spend money on lottery tickets that you can afford to lose.

- Strategies for Sticking to Your Budget:
  Once you've set a budget, it's important to stick to it. One strategy is to allocate a specific amount of cash for lottery tickets each week or month, rather than using credit or debit cards, which can lead to overspending. Additionally, keeping track of your lottery spending over time can help you stay within your budget and make adjustments as needed.

- 1.2 Tailoring Your Budget to Different Lottery Games

Different lottery games require different levels of investment. Tailoring your budget to the specific games you play can help you optimize your spending and improve your chances of winning

- Adjusting Your Budget for Different Games:
  Some lottery games offer better odds than others, while some have larger jackpots. Tailor your budget according to the specific game you're playing. For example, you might allocate a larger portion of your budget to games with better odds or smaller, more frequent prizes, while setting aside a smaller amount for games with massive jackpots but lower chances of winning.

- Budgeting for Syndicate Play vs. Individual Play:
  If you participate in a lottery syndicate, consider how your contribution to the syndicate fits into your overall lottery budget. Syndicate play often involves pooling money with others to purchase more tickets, which can increase your chances of winning but also requires careful budgeting to ensure that you're not overextending yourself.

- **Case Studies of Successful Lottery Budgeting:**
  Look at examples of players who have successfully managed their lottery budgets over time. For instance, some winners consistently allocated a small portion of their income to lottery tickets, never spending more than they could afford. This disciplined approach not only kept their finances in check but also allowed them to continue playing the lottery over the long term without financial stress.

- **1.3 Avoiding Overspending and Financial Pitfalls**

Overspending on lottery tickets is a common problem for many players. Understanding how to avoid this pitfall is crucial for maintaining financial stability and enjoying lottery play responsibly.

- **Recognizing the Signs of Problem Gambling:**
  Problem gambling can start innocuously but escalate quickly if not recognized and addressed. Signs include spending more than you can afford, chasing losses, borrowing money to buy tickets, or feeling anxious and stressed about lottery play. If you notice these behaviors, it's important to take a step back and reassess your approach.

- **Strategies for Reducing Spending:**
  If you find yourself spending more on lottery tickets than you're comfortable with, consider setting stricter limits or taking a break from playing. Another strategy is to participate in a lottery syndicate, where you can still enjoy the thrill of playing but with a smaller financial commitment.

- **Resources for Monitoring Spending:**
  Various tools and resources are available to help you monitor your lottery spending. For example, budgeting apps can track your expenses and provide insights into your spending habits. Additionally, many financial institutions offer tools that categorize your spending, helping you see exactly how much you're spending on lottery tickets each month.

Section 2: Investment Strategies for Lottery Winnings

- **2.1 Planning for Success**

Winning the lottery can lead to financial windfall, but without a plan, it can also lead to financial ruin. It's essential to have an investment plan in place to manage and grow your wealth responsibly.

- **The Importance of an Investment Plan:**
  The first step after winning the lottery is to create a comprehensive investment plan that aligns with your financial goals. This plan should take into account your current financial situation, your future needs, and your risk tolerance. A well-thought-out plan will help you make informed decisions about how to manage and invest your winnings.

- Creating a Financial Plan Before You Win:
  Ideally, you should start thinking about your financial plan even before you win. Consider what you would do with a large sum of money, how you would invest it, and what your long-term financial goals are. This preemptive planning can help you avoid making impulsive decisions if you do win.

- Steps to Take Immediately After Winning:
  If you do win, the first thing to do is take a deep breath and avoid making any immediate decisions. Secure your ticket, seek professional advice, and take the time to develop a clear plan. Consider setting up a trust or legal entity to protect your identity and manage the funds. Begin working with a financial advisor who can guide you through the initial steps of managing your new wealth.

- 2.2 Growing and Protecting Your Wealth

Once you've won, the next challenge is to grow and protect your wealth. This involves smart investing, avoiding risky ventures, and planning for the future.

- Investment Strategies for Lottery Winners:
  A diversified investment strategy is key to growing and protecting your wealth. This might include a mix of stocks, bonds, real estate, and other investment vehicles. The goal is to create a balanced portfolio that can grow over time while minimizing risk.

- Diversifying Your Investments:
  Diversification is the practice of spreading your investments across different asset classes to reduce risk. For example, rather than putting all your money into stocks, you might allocate some to real estate, bonds, or mutual funds. This approach ensures that your wealth is not overly reliant on any single investment and can help protect against market volatility.

- Case Studies of Successful Investment Strategies:
  Learn from other lottery winners who have successfully grown their wealth. For instance, one winner might have invested in a diversified portfolio of stocks and bonds, while another invested in real estate, generating steady income over time. These examples can provide inspiration and guidance for developing your own investment strategy.

- 2.3 Avoiding the Lottery Curse

The "lottery curse" refers to the phenomenon where lottery winners end up losing their fortunes due to poor financial decisions. Avoiding this fate requires discipline, careful planning, and a long-term perspective.

- Understanding the Lottery Curse:
  The lottery curse is often the result of winners making impulsive decisions, such as spending lavishly, making risky investments, or giving away large sums of money without considering the long-term consequences. Understanding this phenomenon is the first step in avoiding it.

- **Strategies for Avoiding Common Mistakes:**
  To avoid the lottery curse, take a disciplined approach to managing your wealth. This includes creating a detailed budget, sticking to your investment plan, and avoiding the temptation to spend recklessly. It's also important to surround yourself with trusted advisors who can help you make informed decisions.

- **The Role of Financial Advisors:**
  A financial advisor can be an invaluable resource for managing your wealth. Choose an advisor who is experienced in handling large sums of money and who understands your financial goals. Regular check-ins with your advisor can help you stay on track and adjust your plan as needed.

Section 3: Understanding the Tax Implications

- **3.1 Tax Responsibilities of Lottery Winners**

One of the first things you'll need to address after winning the lottery is your tax obligations. Understanding how lottery winnings are taxed is crucial to ensuring that you comply with the law and protect your wealth.

- **How Lottery Winnings are Taxed:**
  In most jurisdictions, lottery winnings are considered taxable income. Depending on the amount you win and where you live, you may owe federal, state, and local taxes. It's important to understand the tax rates that apply to your winnings and how they will impact your overall financial situation.

- **Strategies for Minimizing Your Tax Burden:**
  There are several strategies you can use to minimize your tax liability. These might include setting up a trust to manage the funds, making charitable donations, or spreading the winnings over several years. A tax professional can help you explore these options and develop a plan that minimizes your tax burden while ensuring compliance with the law.

- **3.2 Working with Financial Advisors and Tax Professionals**

Given the complexity of managing lottery winnings, it's crucial to work with experienced professionals who can guide you through the process.

- **The Importance of Professional Advice:**
  A financial advisor can help you create a long-term financial plan, while a tax professional can ensure that you meet all your tax obligations. Together, they can help you navigate the challenges of managing a large sum of money and ensure that you're making the most of your winnings.

- 3.2 Working with Financial Advisors and Tax Professionals (continued)

    ### Choosing the Right Experts:
    When selecting financial advisors and tax professionals, it's important to choose individuals who have experience dealing with large sums of money and understand the specific tax laws that apply to lottery winnings. Look for advisors with a strong track record, positive client reviews, and relevant certifications or qualifications. It's also advisable to work with a fiduciary, someone who is legally obligated to act in your best interest.

    ### Building a Trusted Financial Team:
    Your financial team should work together to ensure that your wealth is managed effectively. This might include not only a financial advisor and tax professional but also an estate planner, attorney, and accountant. Regular meetings with your team will help you stay informed and make sure that all aspects of your financial plan are coordinated.

    ### Legal Considerations:
    Depending on your jurisdiction, you may need to consider legal structures such as trusts or limited liability companies (LLCs) to manage your winnings. These structures can provide tax benefits, protect your privacy, and help manage the distribution of your assets. A lawyer specializing in estate planning or tax law can help you set up these structures and ensure that they are legally sound.

- 3.3 Legal Strategies for Managing Large Winnings

Beyond taxes, there are additional legal considerations to manage your wealth and protect your assets.

Setting Up Trusts and LLCs:
One common strategy for managing large lottery winnings is to set up a trust or LLC. These legal entities can provide privacy, limit liability, and help with estate planning. For example, setting up a trust can allow you to control how and when your assets are distributed to beneficiaries, protecting your wealth for future generations.

Estate Planning:
Lottery winnings can significantly impact your estate plan. It's important to review and update your estate plan to reflect your new financial situation. This might include revising your will, setting up trusts, and considering how your wealth will be distributed after your death. Proper estate planning ensures that your assets are passed on according to your wishes and can help minimize estate taxes.

Protecting Your Assets:
Large sums of money can make you a target for lawsuits or fraudulent schemes. Legal strategies such as asset protection trusts can help shield your wealth from potential claims. It's also important to be cautious about sharing information about your winnings and to seek legal advice before making any major financial decisions.

Conclusion of Chapter 5

Financial planning and risk management are critical components of a successful lottery strategy. By setting and sticking to a budget, planning your investments, and understanding the tax and legal implications of winning, you can ensure that your lottery windfall becomes a lasting source of financial security and success.

The key to managing large sums of money is to approach your finances with the same level of discipline and planning that you applied to winning the lottery. With the right team of professionals, a clear financial plan, and a focus on long-term goals, you can avoid the pitfalls that have trapped many lottery winners before you. This chapter has provided you with the tools and strategies needed to navigate the financial challenges that come with sudden wealth, helping you to protect and grow your winnings for years to come.

Chapter 6: Avoiding Common Pitfalls

Introduction to Common Pitfalls in Lottery Play

Even the most experienced lottery players can fall into traps that undermine their chances of success or lead to financial difficulties. These pitfalls range from psychological biases to overspending and mismanaging winnings. This chapter will help you identify and avoid these common mistakes, ensuring that your lottery play remains a positive and rewarding experience.

Section 1: Psychological Insights into Lottery Play

- 1.1 The Psychology of Lottery Play

Understanding the psychological factors that influence lottery behavior is essential for avoiding common mistakes. Many players fall into cognitive traps that can lead to poor decision-making and financial losses.

- Cognitive Biases in Lottery Play:
  Cognitive biases are systematic errors in thinking that can affect lottery players in various ways. For example, the Gambler's Fallacy is the mistaken belief that past lottery outcomes influence future ones. Players might think that if a number hasn't been drawn in a while, it's "due" to be drawn soon, leading them to choose numbers based on this flawed logic.

- Confirmation Bias:
  Another common bias is confirmation bias, where players focus on information that supports their beliefs and ignore evidence to the contrary. For instance, a player who believes in "lucky numbers" might selectively remember when those numbers win and disregard the many times they don't.

- Strategies to Overcome Cognitive Biases:
  The key to overcoming these biases is awareness and education. By understanding that each lottery draw is independent and random, you can avoid falling into the trap of thinking that certain numbers are "due" or "lucky." Instead, base your number selections on sound strategies, such as those discussed in earlier chapters.

- 1.2 Emotional Decision-Making and Its Consequences

Emotions play a significant role in how we make decisions, especially in high-stakes games like the lottery. However, emotional decision-making can lead to irrational choices and poor outcomes.

- The Impact of Excitement and Frustration:
  Winning or losing in the lottery can evoke strong emotions. Excitement after a win might lead you to spend more than you planned, while frustration after a loss might drive you to chase your losses, spending more in an attempt to recover what you lost.

- The Dangers of "Chasing Losses":
  Chasing losses is a common pitfall where players continue to spend money in an attempt to recover what they've lost, often leading to even greater losses. This behavior is particularly dangerous because it can spiral out of control, leading to significant financial harm.

- Techniques for Maintaining Emotional Control:
  To avoid making decisions based on emotion, it's important to establish rules for your lottery play. For example, set a budget and stick to it, regardless of wins or losses. Take breaks between games to avoid impulsive decisions, and remind yourself that the lottery is a game of chance, not a guaranteed way to make money.

- 1.3 The Impact of Stress and Pressure

Stress and external pressure can exacerbate the risks of emotional decision-making, leading to poor choices and unhealthy behaviors.

- How Stress Affects Decision-Making:
  When under stress, people are more likely to make impulsive decisions. This is because stress can impair cognitive function, making it harder to think clearly and evaluate options rationally. In the context of the lottery, stress might lead you to buy more tickets than you can afford or choose numbers based on a hunch rather than a strategy.

- Managing Stress in Lottery Play:
  Managing stress is crucial for maintaining a healthy relationship with the lottery. Techniques such as mindfulness, meditation, or simply taking a break can help reduce stress and improve decision-making. Additionally, setting clear boundaries for your lottery play can help you avoid feeling overwhelmed or pressured.

- The Importance of Taking Breaks:
  Regular breaks from lottery play can help you maintain perspective and avoid burnout. During these breaks, you can reassess your strategy, review your financial situation, and ensure that your lottery play remains a fun and manageable activity.

Section 2: Advanced Strategies to Avoid Overconfidence

- 2.1 The Dangers of Overconfidence

Overconfidence is a common pitfall that can lead to risky behavior and financial losses. Even experienced players can fall into this trap, believing that their past success or knowledge makes them immune to the lottery's inherent randomness.

- Why Overconfidence Happens:
  Overconfidence often arises from past successes. For example, if you've won a few small prizes, you might start to believe that you have a special talent or insight that gives you an edge. This belief can lead to increased spending, riskier bets, and a false sense of control over the game.

- Case Studies of Overconfidence Leading to Losses:
  Many players who initially experienced success have lost significant amounts of money due to overconfidence. For example, a player who wins a mid-sized prize might start buying more tickets or playing more frequently, believing that their "luck" will continue. However, without a sound strategy and an understanding of the game's randomness, this approach often leads to greater losses.

- How to Maintain a Balanced Perspective:
  The key to avoiding overconfidence is to stay grounded and realistic about the lottery's odds. Remember that every draw is independent, and past wins do not influence future outcomes. Regularly review your strategy and spending to ensure that you're not taking unnecessary risks based on overconfidence.

- 2.2 Regularly Reassessing Your Strategy

A successful lottery strategy is one that evolves over time. Regularly reassessing your approach helps you stay adaptable and responsive to changes in the game or your personal situation.

- The Importance of Strategy Evaluation:
  Periodically evaluating your lottery strategy allows you to identify what's working and what's not. This process might involve reviewing your past results, analyzing your spending, and considering any changes in the lottery's rules or structure.

- Adapting to New Information:
  As you learn more about the lottery and gain experience, it's important to adjust your strategy accordingly. This might mean incorporating new techniques, changing your number selection process, or altering your budget based on your financial situation.

- Examples of Successful Strategy Reassessment:
  Consider a player who initially focused on playing a single lottery game but later expanded to include other games with better odds. By reassessing their strategy and adapting to new information, they improved their chances of winning and reduced their overall risk.

- 2.3 Balancing Confidence with Caution

Confidence is important in lottery play, but it must be balanced with caution to avoid reckless behavior.

- The Role of Confidence in Success:
  Confidence can help you stick to your strategy and make decisive choices, but it's important to ensure that your confidence is based on sound reasoning rather than wishful thinking. Confidence should come from a clear understanding of the game's mechanics and a disciplined approach to play.

- Caution as a Counterbalance:
  Caution involves being aware of the risks and taking steps to mitigate them. This might include setting limits on your spending, avoiding high-risk bets, and being prepared to walk away when necessary. By balancing confidence with caution, you can enjoy the excitement of lottery play without exposing yourself to unnecessary risks.

- Strategies for Maintaining a Balanced Approach:
  One way to balance confidence with caution is to establish "safety nets" within your strategy. For example, you might set a limit on how much you're willing to lose in a single month or establish rules for when to stop playing if you're on a losing streak. These safeguards can help you stay in control and avoid the negative consequences of overconfidence.

Section 3: In-Depth Analysis of Gambling Addiction

- 3.1 Recognizing the Signs of Problem Gambling

Gambling addiction is a serious issue that can have devastating effects on your finances, relationships, and overall well-being. Recognizing the signs early is crucial for preventing it from escalating.

- Signs of Problem Gambling:
  Problem gambling can manifest in various ways, such as spending more time and money on the lottery than intended, feeling restless or irritable when not playing, or lying to loved ones about your lottery play. Other signs include chasing losses, neglecting responsibilities, and experiencing financial difficulties due to lottery spending.

- The Difference Between Healthy Play and Addiction:
  It's important to distinguish between healthy lottery play, where the activity is enjoyed responsibly and within limits, and addiction, where the behavior becomes compulsive and harmful. Healthy play involves sticking to a budget, playing for entertainment, and understanding that the lottery is a game of chance.

- Case Studies of Gambling Addiction:
  Many players have struggled with gambling addiction, often starting with seemingly harmless lottery play that gradually escalated. Learning from these cases can help you recognize the early warning signs and take action before the problem worsens.

- 3.2 Strategies for Maintaining Control

Maintaining control over your lottery play is key to preventing gambling addiction and ensuring that the game remains a positive experience.

- Setting Limits:
  One of the most effective ways to maintain control is to set clear limits on your lottery play. This might include a budget for how much you're willing to spend each week or month, as well as a time limit on how long you'll spend playing. Sticking to these limits can help prevent the behavior from becoming compulsive.

Section 3: In-Depth Analysis of Gambling Addiction (continued)

- 3.2 Strategies for Maintaining Control (continued)

    Using Self-Exclusion Tools:
    Many jurisdictions and lottery organizations offer self-exclusion tools that allow you to voluntarily ban yourself from participating in lottery games for a specified period. This can be an effective way to take a break and regain control over your gambling habits if you feel they are becoming problematic.

    The Importance of Monitoring Your Behavior:
    Regularly monitor your behavior and be honest with yourself about how much time and money you're spending on lottery play. If you notice any warning signs of problem gambling, such as spending more than you intended or feeling guilty about your lottery habits, take immediate steps to address the issue.

    Seeking Help Early:
    If you find that you're struggling to control your lottery play, it's important to seek help early. There are many resources available, including counseling services, support groups, and helplines that specialize in gambling addiction. Reaching out for help is a crucial step in preventing a full-blown addiction and getting back on track.

- 3.3 Seeking Help and Support

Recognizing when to seek help is critical in preventing gambling addiction from taking over your life. There is no shame in asking for assistance, and many resources are available to support you.

When to Seek Professional Help:
If you find that you're unable to control your lottery play despite your best efforts, or if it's causing significant distress or financial problems, it's time to seek professional help. This might include therapy, counseling, or joining a support group for individuals with gambling issues.

Types of Support Available:
Various types of support are available for those struggling with gambling addiction. Cognitive-behavioral therapy (CBT) is a common treatment approach that helps individuals identify and change the thought patterns that lead to compulsive gambling. Support groups like Gamblers Anonymous provide a community of peers who understand what you're going through and can offer guidance and encouragement.

Rebuilding After Gambling Addiction:

Recovery from gambling addiction is possible, but it requires commitment and support. Once you've sought help and begun the recovery process, focus on rebuilding your life and finances. This might involve creating a new budget, repairing relationships that may have been damaged by your gambling, and finding healthy hobbies or activities to replace lottery play.

Maintaining a Healthy Relationship with Lottery Play:

If you decide to continue playing the lottery after recovering from gambling addiction, it's essential to approach it with caution and set strict boundaries. Consider working with a financial advisor to create a budget that ensures you only spend what you can afford to lose, and continue using the strategies discussed in this chapter to maintain control over your lottery play.

Conclusion of Chapter 6

Avoiding common pitfalls is crucial to sustaining success in lottery play. By understanding the psychological factors that influence your decisions, staying vigilant against overconfidence, and recognizing the signs of problem gambling, you can maintain a disciplined and healthy approach to playing the lottery. This chapter has provided you with the knowledge and strategies needed to navigate the challenges of lottery play and stay on the path to success.

Maintaining a balanced perspective, regularly reassessing your strategy, and being proactive about managing your emotions and stress levels are key to avoiding the traps that can derail even the most experienced players. Remember, the lottery should be a fun and enjoyable activity, not a source of stress or financial strain. By applying the insights from this chapter, you can ensure that your lottery play remains a positive part of your life.

Chapter 7: Real-Life Stories from Lottery Winners

Introduction to Learning from Lottery Winners

There is much to be learned from the experiences of those who have won the lottery. These real-life stories provide valuable insights into what strategies worked, the challenges winners faced, and the lessons they learned along the way. By analyzing these stories, you can gain a deeper understanding of how to approach your own lottery play, as well as how to manage your winnings wisely if you do hit the jackpot.

Section 1: Analyzing the Success Stories

- 1.1 Case Studies of Big Winners

Studying the experiences of big lottery winners can offer a wealth of knowledge. These case studies highlight the strategies that led to their success and the decisions they made after winning.

- Narratives of Major Wins:
  Consider the story of a couple from Florida who won a $528 million Powerball jackpot. Their approach to winning involved playing regularly with a small, consistent budget and using a mix of personal and random numbers. Upon winning, they sought immediate legal and financial advice, which helped them manage their windfall effectively and avoid many of the pitfalls that have befallen other winners.

- Strategies that Led to Success:
  Many successful lottery winners attribute their wins to a combination of consistent play, strategic number selection, and sheer luck. For example, a group of office workers in Canada won a $60 million jackpot after participating in a workplace lottery pool for several years. Their strategy involved pooling resources to purchase a large number of tickets, which increased their odds of winning.

- The Impact on Their Lives:
  While winning the lottery can bring financial freedom, it also comes with challenges. Some winners, like the Florida couple, chose to remain anonymous to protect their privacy, while others have used their winnings to support charitable causes or invest in their communities. However, not all stories have happy endings, as some winners struggle with the pressures and responsibilities that come with sudden wealth.

- 1.2 Common Traits Among Successful Players

Despite the randomness of lottery outcomes, certain traits are often found among successful lottery players. These traits can serve as valuable lessons for those hoping to improve their chances.

- Discipline and Patience:
  Successful lottery winners often demonstrate a high level of discipline and patience. They set budgets, stick to their strategies, and play consistently over time. Rather than chasing every big jackpot, they focus on games that align with their goals and risk tolerance.

- Pragmatism and Realism:
  Many winners understand that the lottery is a game of chance and approach it with a realistic mindset. They know that winning is not guaranteed and are prepared for the possibility of losing. This pragmatism helps them avoid risky behavior and maintain a healthy perspective on lottery play.

- **Seeking Professional Advice:**
  A common trait among winners who successfully manage their wealth is their willingness to seek professional advice. Whether it's legal, financial, or tax-related, getting expert guidance has helped many winners navigate the complexities of sudden wealth and make informed decisions about their future.

- **1.3 Lessons Learned from Successful Winners**

Analyzing the experiences of successful lottery winners can provide valuable insights into what to do—and what not to do—if you find yourself in a similar position.

- **The Importance of Planning:**
  One of the key lessons from successful winners is the importance of planning. Winners who take the time to plan their next steps—whether it's securing their ticket, consulting with advisors, or deciding how to invest their winnings—tend to fare better in the long run.

- **Avoiding Impulsive Decisions:**
  Sudden wealth can lead to impulsive decisions, such as making large purchases or giving away money without careful consideration. Many winners emphasize the importance of taking a step back, thinking through decisions, and not rushing into anything.

- **Maintaining a Balanced Life:**
  For some winners, the sudden influx of money can disrupt their lives, leading to stress, strained relationships, or even isolation. Successful winners often prioritize maintaining a sense of normalcy, staying connected with friends and family, and balancing their new lifestyle with their previous routines.

Section 2: Learning from Mistakes of Past Winners

- 2.1 The "Lottery Curse": Stories of Winners Who Lost It All

While many lottery winners go on to live comfortable lives, others fall victim to what's known as the "lottery curse." These stories serve as cautionary tales about the risks of mismanaging sudden wealth.

- **Case Studies of the Lottery Curse:**
  Consider the story of a British man who won £10 million but lost it all within a few years due to lavish spending, poor investments, and a series of personal setbacks. Despite his initial excitement, the winner admitted that the money brought more problems than joy, leading to the breakdown of relationships and his eventual bankruptcy.

- Common Pitfalls Leading to Financial Ruin:
  The lottery curse often stems from a lack of financial planning, reckless spending, and poor decision-making. Winners who are unprepared for the responsibilities of managing large sums of money may find themselves overwhelmed, leading to impulsive purchases, bad investments, and legal troubles.

- The Psychological and Emotional Challenges:
  Sudden wealth can also bring psychological and emotional challenges. Some winners struggle with the pressure of managing their money, dealing with newfound attention, or handling requests for financial help from friends and family. These challenges can lead to stress, anxiety, and even depression if not addressed properly.

- 2.2 Avoiding the Pitfalls of Sudden Wealth

To avoid the lottery curse, it's crucial to approach your winnings with caution and a long-term perspective.

- Strategies for Protecting Your Wealth:
  The first step in avoiding financial ruin is to secure your winnings and develop a comprehensive financial plan. This plan should include setting aside money for taxes, creating a budget, and making conservative investments to ensure your wealth grows over time.

- The Importance of Financial Education:
  Many winners who fall into the lottery curse lack basic financial education. Understanding the fundamentals of budgeting, investing, and risk management can help you make informed decisions and avoid the common mistakes that lead to financial ruin.

- Building a Support System:
  Surrounding yourself with trusted advisors, friends, and family can provide the emotional and practical support needed to navigate the challenges of sudden wealth. Having a support system in place can help you stay grounded, make sound decisions, and avoid the pitfalls that have trapped other winners.

- 2.3 The Importance of Planning for the Future

Proper planning is key to ensuring that your lottery winnings lead to long-term financial security and happiness.

- Developing a Long-Term Financial Plan:
  A well-structured financial plan should account for your current needs, future goals, and potential risks. This plan might include investing in a diversified portfolio, setting up trusts or other legal structures to protect your assets, and planning for retirement.

- Estate Planning Considerations:
  Estate planning is an essential aspect of managing large sums of money. Setting up a trust, creating a will, and considering how your wealth will be passed on to future generations can help ensure that your winnings are used in accordance with your wishes and protected from unnecessary taxes and legal challenges.

- The Role of Philanthropy and Giving Back:
  Many winners find fulfillment in using their wealth to give back to their communities or support causes they care about. Philanthropy can be an important part of your financial plan, providing a sense of purpose and helping you make a positive impact with your winnings.

Section 3: Comprehensive Case Studies

- 3.1 Detailed Narratives of Winners and Losers

Examining the stories of both successful and unsuccessful lottery winners can provide valuable lessons and insights.

- Success Stories:
  Take the example of a New York man who won $326 million in the Mega Millions. After winning, he immediately hired a team of financial and legal advisors who helped him create a plan to manage his wealth. He invested wisely, gave to charity, and set up trusts to ensure his family's financial future. His story illustrates the importance of careful planning and seeking professional advice.

- Tragic Tales:
  On the other end of the spectrum, consider the case of a West Virginia man who won $315 million but lost it all within a few years. His story is marked by lavish spending, legal troubles, and personal tragedies, including the loss of his granddaughter. His experience serves as a stark reminder of the dangers of mismanaging wealth and the importance of having a solid financial plan in place.

- 3.2 What Worked, What Didn't, and Why

Analyzing the successes and failures of past winners can help you understand what strategies are most effective and which pitfalls to avoid.

- Key Success Factors:
  Common success factors among lottery winners include disciplined spending, strategic investments, and seeking professional advice. Winners who focused on long-term financial security, rather than short-term gratification, were more likely to maintain and grow their wealth.

- Common Mistakes:
Conversely, common mistakes include impulsive spending, failing to account for taxes, and neglecting to plan for the future. Winners who fell into these traps often found themselves in financial trouble within a few years, despite their initial windfall.

- Lessons for Future Winners:
The experiences of past winners highlight the importance of approaching your winnings with caution, planning carefully, and maintaining a balanced perspective. By learning from their successes and mistakes, you can improve your own chances of turning a lottery win into lasting financial security.

- 3.3 Applying These Lessons to Your Strategy

    Incorporating Success Strategies:

    Consider adopting the strategies that have worked for successful winners. This might include playing the lottery consistently but within a strict budget, seeking professional advice immediately after a win, and creating a detailed financial plan that prioritizes long-term security over short-term gratification. By incorporating these proven strategies, you can increase your chances of not only winning but also managing your winnings wisely.

    Avoiding Common Mistakes:

    Learning from the mistakes of past winners is just as important as emulating their successes. Avoid the pitfalls of impulsive spending, lack of planning, and overconfidence. Instead, approach your winnings with a clear mind and a well-thought-out plan, ensuring that your wealth will last for years to come.

    Developing a Personal Action Plan:

    Based on the lessons from real-life case studies, you can develop a personal action plan tailored to your specific goals and circumstances. This plan should include steps to secure your winnings, consult with professionals, invest wisely, and maintain a balanced lifestyle. By having a clear plan in place, you'll be better prepared to handle the challenges and opportunities that come with a lottery win.

Conclusion of Chapter 7

Real-life stories from lottery winners offer valuable lessons that can guide your own journey as a lottery player. Whether you're learning from the successes of those who have managed their wealth wisely or the mistakes of those who fell victim to the lottery curse, these insights can help you navigate the challenges of sudden wealth.

The experiences of past winners underscore the importance of disciplined spending, strategic planning, and seeking professional advice. By applying the lessons learned from these stories, you can improve your chances of turning a lottery win into a lasting source of financial security and personal fulfillment.

As you continue to play the lottery, keep these stories in mind and use them to inform your strategy. Whether you win big or small, the principles of smart financial management, careful planning, and balanced living will help you make the most of your winnings and avoid the common pitfalls that have trapped others.

Chapter 8: Tools and Resources for Serious Players

Introduction to Tools and Resources

In the world of lottery play, having the right tools and resources at your disposal can significantly enhance your chances of success. From software that helps you analyze numbers to online communities where you can share strategies, these resources are invaluable for serious players. This chapter explores the most effective tools, books, and communities available to help you optimize your lottery strategy.

Section 1: Advanced Software and Tools

- 1.1 Lottery Analysis Software

Lottery analysis software is a powerful tool for players who want to take their strategy to the next level. These programs allow you to analyze past draws, identify patterns, and make data-driven decisions about which numbers to play.

- Overview of Top Software Tools:
  Several lottery analysis programs are widely used by serious players. Tools like Lotto Pro, Lottery Looper, and WinSlips offer features such as number tracking, pattern recognition, and wheeling systems. These programs can analyze vast amounts of data quickly, helping you spot trends that might not be obvious at first glance.

- Features to Look For:
  When choosing lottery software, look for features that align with your strategy. Key features include number frequency analysis, historical draw data, and the ability to generate wheeling systems. Some advanced tools also offer predictive analytics, which use algorithms to suggest numbers based on past performance.

- How to Use Lottery Software Effectively:
  To get the most out of lottery software, it's important to integrate it into your broader strategy. Use the software to track your chosen numbers, identify any patterns or trends, and refine your selection process over time. Regularly update the software with the latest draw results to ensure that your analysis is based on the most current data.

- 1.2 Spreadsheet Tools for Custom Analysis

For players who prefer a more hands-on approach, spreadsheets offer a customizable way to analyze lottery data. Programs like Excel and Google Sheets allow you to create your own models and track your numbers in a way that suits your specific strategy.

- Setting Up a Spreadsheet for Lottery Play:
  Start by creating a spreadsheet that lists past draw results, along with the frequency of each number. You can use functions like COUNTIF and SUM to calculate how often each number has been drawn and identify any patterns. Spreadsheets also allow you to experiment with different strategies, such as wheeling systems or number clustering, and see how they perform over time.

- Customizing Your Analysis:
  The real power of spreadsheets lies in their flexibility. You can create custom formulas to analyze your data in ways that lottery software might not support. For example, you could track the performance of specific number combinations or create a model that adjusts your number selection based on the size of the jackpot.

- **Customizing Your Analysis:**
  The real power of spreadsheets lies in their flexibility. You can create custom formulas to analyze your data in ways that lottery software might not support. For example, you could track the performance of specific number combinations or create a model that adjusts your number selection based on the size of the jackpot.

- **Examples of Effective Spreadsheet Models:**
  Some players use spreadsheets to create complex models that predict future draws based on historical data. For instance, you might build a spreadsheet that tracks the occurrence of "hot" and "cold" numbers over time, or one that analyzes the relationship between jackpot size and ticket sales. By tailoring your analysis to your specific goals, you can gain a deeper understanding of the lottery and improve your chances of winning.

- **1.3 Apps and Mobile Tools**

In today's digital age, mobile apps provide a convenient way to manage your lottery play on the go. These apps offer features such as number tracking, ticket management, and real-time draw results, making it easier than ever to stay on top of your game.

- **The Best Lottery Apps for Serious Players:**
  There are numerous lottery apps available, each offering different features to suit your needs. Popular apps like LotteryHUB, Lotto Results, and Jackpocket provide real-time updates on draw results, allow you to scan and store your tickets, and even offer number generators based on statistical analysis.

- **Integrating Mobile Tools into Your Strategy:**
  Mobile apps are particularly useful for players who want to stay informed and manage their tickets efficiently. Use these apps to set reminders for upcoming draws, track the numbers you've played, and receive notifications if you win. Many apps also offer insights into the odds of different games, helping you make informed decisions about where to focus your efforts.

- **How to Use Mobile Apps for Number Selection:**
  Some lottery apps include number generators or suggest numbers based on historical data. While these tools can be helpful, it's important to integrate them with your broader strategy. Use the app's suggestions as a starting point, but refine your selections based on your own analysis and insights.

Section 2: Expert Recommendations for Further Reading

- 2.1 Essential Books on Lottery Strategies

Books on lottery strategies provide in-depth knowledge and expert advice that can help you refine your approach. These books cover everything from probability theory to practical tips for maximizing your chances of winning.

- Must-Read Books for Serious Players:
  Some of the most respected books in the field include "The Lottery Black Book" by Larry Blair, which offers a system for picking winning numbers, and "Learn How to Increase Your Chances of Winning the Lottery" by Richard Lustig, a seven-time lottery grand prize winner who shares his personal strategy. Another valuable resource is "Lottery Master Guide" by Gail Howard, which delves into the math behind winning strategies.

- Summaries of Key Books:
  "The Lottery Black Book" focuses on identifying patterns in past draws and using them to predict future outcomes. It emphasizes the importance of consistency and discipline in playing the lottery. "Learn How to Increase Your Chances of Winning the Lottery" outlines a systematic approach to number selection and ticket purchasing, based on the author's extensive experience. "Lottery Master Guide" provides a comprehensive overview of various strategies, including wheeling systems, number selection, and bankroll management.

- Using Books to Deepen Your Knowledge:
  Reading these books can help you gain a deeper understanding of the lottery and refine your strategy. Consider taking notes as you read, and experiment with the strategies discussed in the books to see how they work for you. By combining the insights from these books with your own analysis, you can develop a well-rounded approach to playing the lottery.

- 2.2 Articles and Research Papers

For players who enjoy a more academic approach, articles and research papers offer valuable insights into the mathematics and psychology of lottery play.

- Important Articles on Lottery Mathematics:
  Articles on probability theory, combinatorial analysis, and statistical patterns can provide a deeper understanding of how lottery numbers behave. For example, studies on the "Law of Large Numbers" and "Random Number Generation" can shed light on why certain strategies might be more effective than others.

- Where to Find Research on Lottery Strategies:
  Many academic journals and websites publish research on lottery strategies. Websites like JSTOR and Google Scholar offer access to peer-reviewed papers on topics ranging from probability theory to behavioral economics. Additionally, some lottery organizations publish reports on the statistical analysis of their games, which can be a valuable resource for serious players.

- Applying Research to Your Strategy:
  The insights gained from academic research can help you refine your lottery strategy. For example, understanding the principles of combinatorial mathematics can improve your number selection process, while research on cognitive biases can help you avoid common mistakes. By staying informed about the latest research, you can keep your strategy fresh and effective.

- 2.3 Newsletters and Online Publications

Staying up to date with the latest trends and strategies in lottery play is essential for serious players. Subscribing to newsletters and following online publications can help you stay informed and ahead of the competition.

- Recommended Newsletters for Lottery Players:
  Several newsletters cater to lottery enthusiasts, offering tips, strategies, and updates on the latest developments in the world of lotteries. Newsletters like "Lottery Post" and "Smart Luck" provide regular insights into winning strategies, industry news, and analysis of recent draws.

- Online Publications and Blogs:
  Many websites and blogs focus on lottery strategies and news. Sites like "Lottery Critic" and "LottoExpert" offer in-depth reviews of different lottery games, strategies for improving your odds, and interviews with past winners. Following these publications can provide you with a steady stream of new ideas and insights to incorporate into your strategy.

- Using These Resources to Stay Informed:
  Regularly reading newsletters and online publications can help you stay on top of new strategies, changes in lottery rules, and emerging trends. By staying informed, you can continuously refine your approach and improve your chances of winning.

Section 3: Engaging with the Lottery Community

- 3.1 Online Forums and Discussion Boards

Engaging with other lottery players through online forums and discussion boards can be an invaluable way to share strategies, learn from others, and stay motivated.

- Popular Online Communities for Lottery Players:
  Sites like "Lottery Post" and "Reddit's r/lottery" offer active communities where players discuss strategies, share their experiences, and offer advice to one another. These forums are a great place to ask questions, get feedback on your strategy, and stay connected with other players who share your passion for the lottery.

- Benefits of Participating in Online Discussions:
  Engaging with others in online communities allows you to learn from the experiences of other players, stay updated on the latest trends, and find support and encouragement. These communities can also provide insights into new strategies that you might not have considered, helping you refine your approach.

- How to Get the Most Out of Online Communities:
  To get the most out of online forums, actively participate in discussions, ask questions, and share your own experiences. Be open to feedback and consider different perspectives. By contributing to the community, you'll build relationships with other players and gain access to a wealth of collective knowledge.

Section 3: Engaging with the Lottery Community (continued)

- 3.2 Social Media Groups and Influencers

Social media platforms offer another way to connect with the lottery community. Following lottery-focused groups and influencers can keep you informed and inspired.

- Lottery-Focused Social Media Groups:
  Platforms like Facebook, Twitter, and Instagram host numerous groups and pages dedicated to lottery enthusiasts. These groups often share tips, updates on upcoming jackpots, and discussions about strategies. For example, Facebook groups like "Lottery Players United" and "Powerball and Mega Millions Fans" offer a space for members to share their experiences and exchange ideas.

- Following Lottery Influencers:
  Some influencers on social media specialize in lottery strategies and advice. These influencers often share content such as number-picking strategies, lottery news, and stories of past winners. Following these influencers can provide daily inspiration and keep you engaged with the latest trends in lottery play.

- Engaging with Social Media Content:
  To get the most out of social media, actively engage with the content by commenting, sharing, and participating in live discussions or Q&A sessions. By interacting with influencers and group members, you can build a network of like-minded players who share your interest in the lottery.

- 3.3 The Benefits of Peer Learning and Collaboration

Collaborating with other lottery players can significantly enhance your strategy. Peer learning allows you to benefit from the experiences and insights of others, helping you refine your approach and stay motivated.

- Learning from Others' Experiences:
  By discussing strategies with other players, you can gain insights into what works and what doesn't. For example, if a member of your lottery community shares a strategy that has led to small but consistent wins, you might consider incorporating elements of that strategy into your own approach.

- Collaborative Strategies and Syndicates:
  In addition to learning from others, some lottery players choose to collaborate by forming syndicates or pooling resources. These collaborative strategies can increase your chances of winning by allowing you to purchase more tickets or cover more combinations than you could on your own. Syndicates also offer the opportunity to share the thrill of playing and winning with others.

- **Maintaining Motivation and Accountability:**
  Being part of a lottery community can help you stay motivated and committed to your strategy. Regularly engaging with other players keeps you focused and accountable, ensuring that you stick to your budget and follow through on your plans. Additionally, the support and encouragement of your peers can make the experience more enjoyable and rewarding.

Conclusion of Chapter 8

The right tools and resources can greatly enhance your ability to play the lottery strategically and effectively. By utilizing advanced software, staying informed through expert literature, and engaging with the lottery community, you can continually improve your approach and stay ahead of the competition.

This chapter has provided a comprehensive list of resources that will support your journey as a serious lottery player. Whether you're analyzing numbers with specialized software, learning from books and research papers, or collaborating with other players online, these tools and resources are essential for refining your strategy and maximizing your chances of winning.

As you move forward, remember to stay curious and open to new ideas. The lottery landscape is always evolving, and by staying engaged with the latest tools and resources, you can keep your strategy fresh and effective.

Chapter 9: Preparing for the Win

Introduction to Preparing for a Lottery Win

Winning the lottery is a life-changing event that brings with it a mix of excitement, responsibility, and potential challenges. While it's easy to focus on the thrill of the win, it's equally important to prepare for what comes next. Proper planning can help you protect your newfound wealth, make informed decisions, and ensure that your lottery winnings bring long-term benefits. This chapter provides a comprehensive guide to the steps you should take immediately after winning, as well as strategies for managing your wealth and navigating the challenges of sudden financial success.

Section 1: Immediate Steps to Take After Winning

- 1.1 Securing the Ticket

The first and most crucial step after realizing you've won the lottery is to secure your winning ticket. This simple piece of paper is your key to millions, and losing it could mean losing your entire prize.

- How to Safeguard Your Ticket:
  Once you've confirmed that you hold a winning ticket, take immediate steps to protect it. This might include signing the back of the ticket, taking a photo of it, and placing it in a secure location, such as a safe or a locked drawer. If possible, consider using a safety deposit box to store the ticket until you're ready to claim your prize.

- Legal Considerations:
  In some jurisdictions, signing your ticket may be required to establish ownership, but it's also a good practice to ensure that no one else can claim your winnings. You may also want to make copies of the ticket, but be aware that some lottery rules stipulate that only the original ticket is valid for claiming the prize.

- Consulting with Legal Counsel:
  Before taking any further steps, it's wise to consult with a lawyer who specializes in lottery wins. They can provide guidance on how to protect your ticket, whether to remain anonymous (if allowed in your jurisdiction), and how to plan your next steps. This initial consultation can help you avoid costly mistakes and ensure that you're fully prepared to claim your winnings.

- 1.2 Assembling Your Financial Team

Winning a significant lottery prize requires professional financial management. Assembling a team of experts can help you navigate the complexities of sudden wealth.

- Key Members of Your Financial Team:
  Your financial team should include an attorney, an accountant, and a financial advisor. Each of these professionals plays a crucial role in managing your winnings:

  - **Attorney:** Your lawyer can help you with legal matters, including the establishment of trusts, managing privacy concerns, and ensuring that you comply with all legal requirements when claiming your prize.

  - **Accountant:** An accountant with experience in managing large sums of money can assist with tax planning, ensuring that you meet all tax obligations while minimizing your tax liability.

  - **Financial Advisor:** A financial advisor can help you develop a long-term plan for managing and growing your wealth, taking into account your financial goals, risk tolerance, and future needs.

- How to Choose Trustworthy Advisors:
  Selecting the right professionals is critical. Look for individuals with a proven track record, relevant certifications, and experience in handling large amounts of money. It's also important to choose advisors who are fiduciaries, meaning they are legally obligated to act in your best interest.

- Establishing Clear Communication:
  Once you've assembled your team, ensure that there is clear communication between all members. Regular meetings and updates are essential to make sure everyone is on the same page and working toward your financial goals.

- 1.3 Managing Publicity and Protecting Your Privacy

Winning the lottery can bring unwanted attention. Managing publicity and protecting your privacy are key steps in ensuring your peace of mind and security.

- The Risks of Publicity:
  Publicity can lead to a range of challenges, including unwanted attention from the media, unsolicited requests for money, and even potential security risks. It's important to carefully consider how much information you want to disclose about your win and to whom.

- Legal Options for Remaining Anonymous:
  In some jurisdictions, lottery winners have the option to remain anonymous. If this is possible in your area, consider taking advantage of this option to protect your privacy. Your attorney can help you navigate the legal process to ensure that your identity remains confidential.

- Strategies for Managing Media Inquiries:
  If you do decide to go public with your win, it's important to have a plan for managing media inquiries. This might include issuing a single statement through your lawyer or financial advisor, rather than giving multiple interviews. Limiting your public appearances can help you maintain control over your personal life and avoid the stress that can come with sudden fame.

Section 2: Protecting Your Wealth

- 2.1 Setting Up Legal Structures

One of the most effective ways to protect your lottery winnings is by setting up legal structures such as trusts or LLCs. These entities can provide a range of benefits, including privacy, tax advantages, and protection from creditors.

- The Benefits of Trusts and LLCs:
  Setting up a trust allows you to control how your assets are distributed, both during your lifetime and after your death. Trusts can also help reduce estate taxes and protect your assets from legal claims. Similarly, an LLC can provide liability protection and help manage your investments in a tax-efficient manner.

- Working with Your Attorney:
  Your attorney will play a key role in setting up these legal structures. They can advise you on the best options for your situation and handle the necessary paperwork. It's important to understand the implications of each structure and ensure that it aligns with your overall financial plan.

- The Importance of Estate Planning:
  Estate planning is a critical component of protecting your wealth. This involves creating a will, setting up trusts, and considering how your assets will be passed on to future generations. Proper estate planning ensures that your wealth is distributed according to your wishes and can help minimize taxes and legal challenges.

- 2.2 Avoiding Common Financial Pitfalls

Sudden wealth can be overwhelming, and many lottery winners make mistakes that lead to financial difficulties. Avoiding these pitfalls is essential to preserving your wealth.

- The Dangers of Overspending:
  One of the most common mistakes lottery winners make is overspending. It's easy to feel like you have endless resources, but without a budget and a long-term plan, your wealth can quickly dwindle. To avoid this, work with your financial advisor to create a budget that accounts for your current lifestyle, future goals, and potential risks.

- Risky Investments:
  Another common pitfall is making risky investments without fully understanding the potential downsides. While it's important to grow your wealth, it's equally important to protect it. Avoid high-risk investments and speculative ventures, especially in the early stages of managing your winnings. Instead, focus on building a diversified portfolio that balances growth with security.

- 2.3 Creating a Long-Term Financial Plan

A long-term financial plan is essential for ensuring that your lottery winnings provide lasting security and stability. This plan should take into account your current needs, future goals, and potential risks.

- Setting Financial Goals:
  Start by setting clear financial goals for the short, medium, and long term. These might include paying off debt, purchasing a home, saving for retirement, and supporting charitable causes. Your financial advisor can help you prioritize these goals and create a plan to achieve them.

- Building a Diversified Investment Portfolio:
  A diversified investment portfolio is the cornerstone of long-term financial security. This might include a mix of stocks, bonds, real estate, and other assets. The goal is to balance risk and reward, ensuring that your wealth continues to grow while being protected from market volatility.

- Regularly Reviewing and Updating Your Plan:
  Your financial plan should be a living document that evolves over time. Regularly review your plan with your financial advisor to ensure that it remains aligned with your goals and reflects any changes in your financial situation or the market.

Section 3: Planning for the Future

- 3.1 Sustaining Your Wealth Over Time

Maintaining your wealth requires ongoing management and discipline. By focusing on sustainability, you can ensure that your winnings continue to provide financial security for years to come.

- The Importance of Financial Discipline:
  Financial discipline is key to sustaining your wealth. This means sticking to your budget, avoiding unnecessary risks, and making decisions based on long-term goals rather than short-term desires. Your financial advisor can help you stay on track and make informed choices that support your financial future.

- Strategies for Growing Your Wealth:
  In addition to protecting your wealth, it's important to focus on growing it over time. This might involve reinvesting dividends, exploring new investment opportunities, or expanding your portfolio. The goal is to ensure that your wealth continues to grow, even in the face of inflation and other economic challenges.

- Avoiding the "Lottery Curse":
  The "lottery curse" refers to the phenomenon where lottery winners lose their wealth due to poor financial decisions or mismanagement. Avoiding this curse requires a disciplined approach to wealth management, as well as a commitment to learning and adapting your strategy over time.

- 3.2 Philanthropy and Giving Back

Many lottery winners find fulfillment in using their wealth to give back to their communities or support causes they care about. Philanthropy can be a meaningful way to make a positive impact with your winnings.

- 3.2 Philanthropy and Giving Back (continued)

    The Role of Philanthropy in Wealth Management:
    Philanthropy not only allows you to make a positive difference but can also be an important part of your overall financial strategy. Charitable giving can provide tax benefits, help you establish a legacy, and offer personal satisfaction. Consider setting up a charitable foundation or making regular donations to causes you're passionate about.

    Creating a Giving Strategy:
    Work with your financial advisor to create a giving strategy that aligns with your values and financial goals. This might include setting up a donor-advised fund, contributing to charities on an ongoing basis, or making significant one-time donations. A well-thought-out giving strategy ensures that your contributions have a lasting impact while fitting into your overall financial plan.

    Examples of Successful Philanthropy:
    Many lottery winners have used their wealth to make substantial contributions to society. For example, some have funded scholarships, supported medical research, or contributed to local community projects. These examples can inspire you to think about how you might use your winnings to give back and leave a positive legacy.

- 3.3 Preparing for the Next Generation

If you have a family, planning for the future includes preparing to pass on your wealth to the next generation. Estate planning and financial education are key components of ensuring that your wealth is preserved and used wisely by your heirs.

Estate Planning Essentials:
Estate planning involves creating a will, setting up trusts, and making decisions about how your assets will be distributed after your death. Proper estate planning ensures that your wishes are carried out, and it can help minimize estate taxes and avoid legal disputes among your heirs.

Educating the Next Generation:
Preparing your children or other heirs to manage their inheritance responsibly is crucial. Consider involving them in financial planning discussions and providing them with financial education to ensure they understand the importance of managing money wisely. This preparation can help prevent the common issues that arise when heirs are unprepared to handle large sums of money.

Using Trusts to Protect Your Legacy:
Trusts can be an effective way to manage how your wealth is distributed over time. For example, you might set up a trust that provides your children with a steady income while preserving the principal for future generations. Trusts can also include stipulations that encourage responsible financial behavior, such as requiring heirs to meet certain criteria before receiving their inheritance.

- 3.4 Building a Lasting Legacy

Beyond financial wealth, many lottery winners aspire to build a lasting legacy that reflects their values and achievements. This might include philanthropy, supporting community projects, or creating a family foundation.

Defining Your Legacy:
Take time to think about the legacy you want to leave behind. This might involve contributing to causes you care about, supporting future generations through education and mentorship, or establishing a foundation that continues to make a difference long after you're gone.

Incorporating Your Legacy into Your Financial Plan:
Work with your financial advisor to incorporate your legacy goals into your overall financial plan. This might involve setting aside funds for charitable endeavors, creating a family foundation, or making investments that align with your values. By planning ahead, you can ensure that your legacy is carried out according to your wishes.

Celebrating and Sharing Your Success:
As you build your legacy, consider how you might share your success with others in a way that inspires and empowers them. This could involve writing a memoir, giving talks, or simply sharing your experiences with family and friends. Celebrating your success and the impact you've made can be a fulfilling way to reflect on your journey and inspire others to pursue their own goals.

Conclusion of Chapter 9

Preparing for a lottery win involves more than just financial planning—it requires a holistic approach that considers your future, your family, and the legacy you want to leave behind. By taking the time to secure your ticket, assemble a financial team, and plan for the long term, you can ensure that your winnings bring lasting benefits.

This chapter has provided a roadmap for navigating the challenges and opportunities that come with sudden wealth. From protecting your privacy and managing publicity to creating a long-term financial plan and building a lasting legacy, the steps you take now will determine the impact of your winnings on your life and the lives of others.

As you move forward, remember that preparation is key. By being proactive and thoughtful in your approach, you can turn your lottery win into a source of security, fulfillment, and positive impact for years to come.

Chapter 10: Conclusion and Final Thoughts

Summary of Key Strategies

As we conclude this book, it's essential to revisit the key strategies and insights that have been discussed throughout the chapters. The journey of a serious lottery player is one of discipline, strategy, and continuous learning. By understanding the mechanics of the lottery, analyzing historical data, selecting numbers strategically, and managing your finances prudently, you can significantly enhance your chances of success and ensure that any winnings are managed wisely.

- Understanding Lottery Mechanics:
  The foundation of any successful lottery strategy lies in a deep understanding of how the game works. From the randomness of number draws to the influence of jackpot sizes on player behavior, mastering the mechanics allows you to approach the lottery with a well-informed perspective. Knowledge of statistical independence, odds calculation, and the various types of lottery games sets the stage for informed decision-making.

- Analyzing Historical Data:
  Historical data analysis provides insights into patterns and trends that can inform your number selection strategy. While the lottery is inherently random, studying past draws, frequency analyses, and number clustering can help you identify potential strategies that align with your goals. The key is to use this data as a guide rather than a guarantee, balancing it with other approaches.

- Advanced Number Selection Strategies:
  The process of selecting lottery numbers is more than just picking random digits. By employing strategies such as wheeling systems, combinatorial math, and risk-reward balancing, you can optimize your number choices. These methods help you cover more combinations, increase your chances of winning smaller prizes, and maintain a disciplined approach to playing the lottery.

- Maximizing Your Chances with Group Play:
  Group play or syndicates offer a powerful way to increase your odds of winning without significantly increasing your financial risk. By pooling resources with others, you can purchase more tickets and cover more combinations. However, successful syndicates require clear agreements, legal considerations, and strategic management to ensure that all members benefit fairly.

- Financial Planning and Risk Management:
  Winning the lottery is just the beginning of a new financial journey. Proper financial planning and risk management are crucial to ensuring that your winnings provide long-term security and success. Setting a budget, creating a diversified investment portfolio, and working with financial professionals are essential steps in managing your wealth responsibly.

- Avoiding Common Pitfalls:
  Even experienced players can fall into traps that undermine their chances of success. Overconfidence, emotional decision-making, and problem gambling are risks that every player must manage. By staying disciplined, reassessing your strategy regularly, and seeking help when needed, you can avoid these pitfalls and maintain a healthy relationship with lottery play.

- Learning from Real-Life Stories:
  The experiences of past lottery winners offer valuable lessons in both success and failure. By studying the stories of those who have won big, you can learn what strategies worked, what mistakes to avoid, and how to navigate the challenges of sudden wealth. These stories remind us that winning the lottery is just one part of the journey; managing the win is where true success lies.

- Utilizing Tools and Resources:
  The right tools and resources can make a significant difference in your lottery strategy. From advanced software and mobile apps to books, articles, and online communities, staying informed and engaged with the latest tools will keep your strategy sharp and effective. Engaging with the lottery community also provides support, motivation, and new ideas that can enhance your approach.

- Preparing for the Win:
  Finally, preparing for the win involves more than just claiming your prize. It requires a comprehensive approach that includes securing your ticket, assembling a financial team, managing publicity, and planning for the future. By taking these steps, you can ensure that your lottery winnings lead to lasting financial security, fulfillment, and a positive legacy.

Reinforcing the Importance of Strategy

As we've explored throughout this book, the lottery is not just a game of chance; it's also a game of strategy. While luck plays a significant role, the decisions you make can influence your chances of success. This is why it's crucial to approach lottery play with a well-thought-out strategy that balances risk and reward, uses data and tools effectively, and is flexible enough to adapt to new information and changing circumstances.

- The Role of Discipline:
  Discipline is the cornerstone of a successful lottery strategy. Whether it's sticking to your budget, consistently applying your chosen strategy, or avoiding emotional decisions, discipline ensures that you stay on track and make informed choices. It's easy to get caught up in the excitement of big jackpots, but maintaining discipline helps you keep your long-term goals in focus.

- **Adapting and Evolving Your Strategy:**
  The lottery landscape is constantly evolving, and so should your strategy. Whether it's a change in the lottery's format, new research that offers fresh insights, or personal experiences that teach valuable lessons, staying adaptable is key to maintaining an effective strategy. Regularly reassessing your approach and being open to new ideas ensures that you remain competitive and ready to seize opportunities.

- **Balancing Risk and Reward:**
  Every lottery strategy involves a balance of risk and reward. High-risk strategies may offer the potential for big wins, but they also come with a greater chance of losses. Conversely, low-risk strategies may lead to smaller, more consistent wins but require patience and persistence. Finding the right balance for your personal situation and goals is crucial to long-term success.

Encouragement to Stay Disciplined and Informed

The journey of a serious lottery player is one of continuous learning and growth. By staying disciplined, informed, and engaged, you can improve your chances of success and ensure that your lottery play remains a positive and rewarding experience.

- **The Value of Continuous Learning:**
  The lottery is a complex game with many nuances, and there is always more to learn. Whether it's reading books on lottery strategies, studying historical data, or engaging with the lottery community, staying informed is key to refining your approach and staying ahead of the competition. The more you learn, the better equipped you'll be to make smart decisions and adapt to changes in the game.

- **Maintaining a Healthy Relationship with the Lottery:**
  It's important to remember that the lottery should be a source of enjoyment, not stress. By maintaining a healthy relationship with the game—one that is disciplined, informed, and balanced—you can ensure that your lottery play enhances your life rather than detracts from it. Set limits, stick to your strategy, and approach the lottery with a mindset of fun and curiosity.

- **Final Thoughts on Winning:**
  Winning the lottery is a dream for many, but it's important to approach it with the right mindset. If you're fortunate enough to win, remember that the real challenge lies in managing your winnings wisely and ensuring that they bring long-term benefits. By planning carefully, seeking professional advice, and staying true to your values, you can turn a lottery win into a lasting source of security and fulfillment.

Looking Forward

As you move forward in your journey as a lottery player, keep in mind the strategies, insights, and lessons discussed in this book. Whether you're playing for fun, dreaming of a big win, or looking to improve your odds, the key is to approach the lottery with a strategic mindset, stay disciplined, and continuously refine your approach.

- Your Journey as a Lottery Player:
  Whether you're new to lottery play or a seasoned veteran, this book has equipped you with the tools and knowledge to enhance your chances. Remember that the lottery is a marathon, not a sprint. Success comes to those who are patient, persistent, and strategic.

- Encouragement for the Future:
  Stay positive, stay disciplined, and keep applying what you've learned. The lottery is unpredictable, but with the right strategy, your chances can improve over time. Above all, enjoy the journey and the excitement that comes with playing the lottery. Wishing you success in your lottery endeavors and beyond.

Closing Remarks

Thank you for taking the time to read this book and invest in your lottery strategy. The road to success in lottery play is long and requires patience, discipline, and a strategic mindset. By applying the lessons and techniques outlined in this book, you've taken a significant step toward improving your chances and preparing for the win of a lifetime.

Remember, winning the lottery is just the beginning. What you do with your winnings, how you manage your wealth, and the legacy you create are what truly define success. Best of luck in your future lottery endeavors, and may your journey be filled with excitement, success, and fulfillment.

Printed in Dunstable, United Kingdom

63618827R00045